LIBRA

HOROSCOPE

& ASTROLOGY

2021

Published by Mystic Cat Press

Suite SM-2380-6403

14601 North Bybee Lake Court

Portland, Oregon 97203

Phone: +1 (805) 308-6503

SiaSands@hotmail.com

Copyright © 2020 by Mystic Cat Press

The information accessible from this book is for informational purposes only. None of the data within should be regarded as a promise of benefits, a statutory warranty, or a guarantee of results to be achieved.

Images are used under license from Fotosearch & Dreamstime.

Contents

January   22

February   28

March   34

April   40

May   46

June   52

July   58

August   64

September   70

October   76

November   83

December   89

Acknowledgment:

To my family, thank you for being there and accepting my wildness.

This book is dedicated to those with an open heart, an open mind, and a willingness to plumb the mysteries of life.

You make this world a better place.

LIBRA 2021
HOROSCOPE & ASTROLOGY

Libra

Libra Dates: September 23 to October 22
Symbol: Scales
Element: Air
Planet: Venus
House: Seventh
Colors: Ivory, pink, light-blue

2021 LIBRA OVERVIEW

2021 inspires and delights with three gorgeous Supermoons in the first half of the year. New opportunities arrive, which will breathe fresh air into your surroundings. Exciting joint projects are likely, this sees your social circle expanding, and offers many opportunities to embrace happiness and connection in your life. You have much to look forward to if you choose this direction. Communication with others is vital in allowing this potential to unfold. You enter an extended time that highlights improved communication and opportunities that expose you to new ideas, people, knowledge, and activities. Unique and inspiring options are revealed in 2021.

On February 12th, we ring in the Chinese New Year of the Ox, this is an important event, the magic, arrives to allow you the ability to harness the power of manifestation. You seek mind-expanding adventures and focus on self-development to inspire you to reach a higher level of achievement. Putting your mental well-being on the front burner pays dividends in future growth. This event is the impetus that creates positive change in your life.

Mercury Retrograde gets up to tricks in 2021, you are especially sensitive to cosmic vibrations, and you begin to feel some cosmic fallout. This is a time of self-assessment and re-balancing. You are being asked to step back from your life to get a better perspective. You may want to take some time out for this reflection or go within through meditation. The key is to embrace a stiller, lower, quieter vibe that allows your deeper knowing to pour forth, allowing you to align with your soul path and purpose, not your ego and its temporary concerns.

LUNAR & SOLAR

Solar eclipses can only occur during a New Moon phase. This is when the Moon moves between Earth and the Sun, and these three celestial bodies form a straight line: Earth–Moon–Sun.

A Lunar eclipse occurs when the earth stands between the moon and the Sun, this obscures the light of the Sun from the moon. The moon herself has no light source of her own, as she simply reflects the light of the Sun. A lunar eclipse occurs during a Full Moon and usually marks endings, transitions, or other life cycle culmination points.

Any eclipse is a significant event in astrological circles, eclipses have fascinated scientists for centuries. Eclipses are dramatic tools that instigate change in your life. An eclipse is wild, free, expansive, and explosive, the wild cards of astrology, you never quite know what you get until it happens. An eclipse can uproot, surprise, inspire, motivate, and really become an active catalyst for change. Eclipses remove the shutters, they make you aware of areas that need to be changed and often spotlight an entirely new direction to explore. Eclipses inspire change and work rapidly to see forward motion occurring.

WORKING WITH THE MOON

2021 delights with three gorgeous Supermoon's. A supermoon is when the moon is at its closest approach to Earth, which occurs during a full or new moon. The effect on the ocean's tides is most significant when there is a full or new moon. This tidal force is concentrated during the super moon, it can cause the ocean tides to rise by an extra inch or two compared to a regular full moon. Super moons are they invite you to look at your life, to reveal areas which you usually keep hidden. High in the night sky, they illuminate a great deal of information should you choose to work with this sacred energy. Connecting with this information gives you a fantastic opportunity to expand your life, to reveal areas that are ready to be developed.

As the moon peaks, it naturally begins to wane, and as the moon heads towards the next gravitational peak, the new moon phase, it has a cleansing effect on your emotional awareness. This helps you remove from your life all the things that need to be released, the areas which limit progress said no real good while they are kept within your spirit. Heading into the new moon gives your excellent opportunity to connect with the mysterious darkness. It is a healing time that brings a powerful sense of cleansing. This removes the outworn energy and makes space for new opportunities to flow into your world as the moon fills once again into a full shining globe.

PLANETARY RETROGRADES

The Retrograde phase is when a planet appears, when observed from Earth, to reverse direction. This happens due to an optical illusion caused by differences in orbit. The retrograde motion can have a negative influence on your life. The planet Mercury is the best-known planet for retrograde phases. This is because Mercury is the fastest planet in our solar system, and it enters a retrograde motion between three to four times a year, for about three weeks at a time. Mercury is a planet that rules communication, so you can expect frequent misunderstandings, scheduling problems, and disagreements during a Mercury Retrograde phase. Here is a quick reference guide to the retrogrades in 2021.

MERCURY: 3 RETROGRADES IN 2021

VENUS: 1 RETROGRADE IN 2021

MARS: NO RETROGRADE IN 2021

JUPITER: 1 RETROGRADE IN 2021

SATURN: 1 RETROGRADE IN 2021

URANUS: 2 RETROGRADE IN 2021

NEPTUNE: 1 RETROGRADE IN 2021

PLUTO: 1 RETROGRADE IN 2021

NODE: 1 RETROGRADE IN 2021

LILITH: NO RETROGRADE IN 2021

CHIRON: 1 RETROGRADE IN 2021

2021

LIBRA HOROSCOPE

Four Weeks Per Month

- Week 1 – Days 1 - 7
- Week 2 – Days 8 - 14
- Week 3 – Days 15 - 21
- Week 4 – Days 22 – Month-end

Time is set to Coordinated Universal Time Zone (UT±0)

January 3, 4 - Quadrantids Meteor Shower.

The Quadrantids meteor shower run yearly from January 1-5. The Quadrantids meteor shower peaks this year on the night of the 3rd and morning of the 4th.

January 6 – Last Quarter Moon in Libra.

This Moon phase occurs at 09.37 UTC.

January 13 – New Moon in Capricorn.

This new moon phase occurs at 05:02 UTC. This cleans the slate and brings a fresh start. This is an excellent time to view galaxies and stars as there is no moonlight to obscure your view of the universe.

January 20 – First Quarter Moon in Aries.

This Moon phase occurs at 21.02 UTC.

January 24 – Mercury at Greatest Eastern Elongation.

The planet Mercury reaches greatest eastern elongation of 18.6 degrees from the Sun. This occurs at 02.00 UTC. Look for Mercury low in the sky just after sunset.

January 28 - Full Moon in Leo.

This phase occurs at 19:16 UTC. Full Wolf Moon. It has also been known as the Old Moon and the Moon After Yule. The Full Moon illuminates and draws new options to light.

January 29 – Jupiter in Conjunction with the Sun.

The planet Jupiter in Conjunction with the Sun. This occurs at 01:00 UTC.

January 30 – Mercury Retrograde begins in Aquarius.

During a retrograde period, it isn't the right time to move forward in any practical venture. Be prepared for misunderstandings and miscommunications to be prevalent.

The Quadrantids Meteor Shower blazes across the night sky this week. You may find that a lot is going on in your life, it is a time that can feel restless. If you feel lower than usual, it is essential to focus on maintaining balance and integrating change into your life so that you move forward in a grounded fashion. Positive energy is ready to emerge, taking time to explore the possibilities brings a golden opportunity. Improvements are indicated, this elevates the potential possible. Opportunity is knocking at your door, and paying heed to signs and synchronicity does let the path ahead open wide with refreshing potential. You no longer need the put the brakes on your life, areas that prevent progress can be resolved. It does put you on a path that holds the promise of an exciting journey forward. A piece of the puzzle is set to be revealed, it brings insight into an area that offers a room to progress your life. In relates to a decision that clears the path ahead. This helps you release doubt and anxiety, you make the right choice for your life and can embrace a grounded and balanced chapter. It does bring an environment that strengthens your life in beautiful ways. Change is available; you step out on a new adventure and harness a sense of excitement. It does reap great rewards as it is a path that harnesses creativity to stunning effect. It does bring options that offer room to grow your world. Immersing yourself in learning a new area does bring dividends. It is essential to be open to the potential that seeks to blossom in your life

JANUARY WEEK TWO

The New Moon in Capricorn at the week's end brings news. You are entering an active phase that revolutionizes your identity and broadens your mind with concepts that epitomize a new attitude to life. You can release any anxiety and focus on the abundance that currently surrounds your life. You find an outlet for your restless energy that provides you with attractive benefits. It encourages a sense of adventure and a willingness to engage in areas of life that radiate limitless potential. Taking a big picture view is best at this time, in the long run, you will see things work out for the best. Taking the time to plan for future contingencies enables you to move forward sustainably. As you connect with your vision, you can make sure it is in alignment with the correct path ahead. Being flexible and maintaining a balance is essential during this delicate chapter. There is magic available in your world, harnessing the power of creativity does bring tangible results. A new project sparks your imagination, this venture arrives to kickstart an original path. It's an ideal time for setting intentions and planning to achieve your aspirations. Structuring goals and going after your dreams does create space necessary to plot the course forward. As you refine and streamline the path ahead, you see your talents growing exponentially. It is a time that gets you back to basics. You are resilient and able to navigate past hurdles and achieve a robust result. Currently, you are on a mission to deliver a fabulous result. Your willingness to explore innovative options does bring new possibilities to light. A healthy dose of optimism lights the path forward. It is instrumental in restoring equilibrium during an uncertain time.

News arrives that delivers a stunning revelation. Watch for a sign that provides an important clue; it guides you towards a new opportunity that lets you transition to a happy chapter. It does seem curious news arrives, which provides an exciting path forward. It brings inspiration flowing into your world and lets you set your sights on a lofty goal. Essential changes are arriving that bring sparkling energy, it gives you the option to improve your situation. Your creativity is ready to be reawakened, nothing dampens your curious appetite over the coming weeks. It does attract new pathways that entice you forward. Investing your energy wisely does see a return soon flow into your world. It brings a time of releasing the blocks and recapturing your sense of adventure. Prospects are coming that expand your creative talents, it does put you in an environment where you can dabble in the arts. You enter an enterprising chapter that brings a remarkable change into view. It does fit perfectly into your life of enlightenment and personal growth. It brings consistency, certainty, and balance into your environment. Your perspective widens, and it brings opportunities for creative brainstorming that lets you choose how you deal with any troubling issues. It does mark a time that flows beautifully forward. This brings a sense of rejuvenation and relaxation that nurtures your spirit. Any minor problems soon resolve as it brings an enriching phase where you plot a course towards growth and self-development. It also suggests a time of turning inwards and reflecting on the changes which surround your life. There is a note of intensity and intrigue that offers a spiritual aspect.

JANUARY WEEK FOUR

Jupiter goes into Conjunction with the Sun the day after the Full Moon in Leo. Jupiter rules luck, growth, wisdom, and fortune. Life gets a boost from this cosmic alignment, it is a time of releasing the blocks, letting go of areas that no longer have a hold on your awareness. You may feel extra sensitive as your situation is going through some growing pains. A significant improvement arrives to point you in the right direction. It brings a serendipitous chapter of personal growth that may involve broadening your perspective and harnessing a mindset that breaks free of limitations. A radical overhaul brings new potential into your life. It does see motivation climbing, and this brings refreshing rejuvenation. A gateway opens that gives you a direction to channel your energy into. It does bring a catalyst for change, it has you taking a leap of faith on a journey forward.

Mercury Retrograde begins in Aquarius at weeks end. You can navigate through this unsettling phase by keeping focused on the destination. Delay unnecessary deals, it's not the best time to sign any legal documents. You also discover areas that are therapeutic for your spirit. This heals wounds that may be holding you back from achieving your best. It does involve a time of nurturing the magic within. It is a time that lets you draw new opportunities into your world. A restless vibe may have you searching for a path that speaks to your spirit. It does bring a journey that gives you space to rejuvenate and renew your spirit. This is an ideal time for setting intentions and exploring new pathways towards growth. A compelling journey opens that illuminates exciting changes ahead.

FEBRUARY ASTROLOGY

February 2 – Imbolc

Harness the element of fire to create something new. Inspiration, motivation, and creativity are rising. The earth is waking after winter's long sleep.

February 4 – Last Quarter Moon in Scorpio.

This Moon phase occurs at 17.37 UTC.

February 8 – Mercury at Inferior Conjunction.

The planet Mercury at Inferior Conjunction. This occurs at 14:00 UTC.

February 11 - New Moon in Aquarius.

This phase occurs at 19:06 UTC. This is an excellent time to view galaxies and stars as there is no moonlight to obscure your view of the universe. This is a time of rebirth and renewal. Create space for something new to arrive.

February 12 – Chinese New Year (Ox)

February 19 – First Quarter Moon in Taurus.

This Moon phase occurs at 18.47 UTC.

February 21 – Mercury Retrograde ends in Aquarius.

You can now move forward with any delayed plans that you have been putting off due to the Mercury Retrograde phase. Relationships should soon improve as miscommunications are overcome

February 27 - Full Moon in Virgo.

The Moon is on the opposite side of the Earth as the Sun and will be fully illuminated. This phase occurs at 08:17 UTC. This full moon is known as the Full Snow Moon. Powerful energy lights a path forward. You can attract and manifest excellent results during the complete moon phase.

You come up with a great idea to while away time spent on the home front. It does draw a fruitful time that explores a path that is off the beaten track. It involves seeking an outlet for the excess of creative energy that is burning within your spirit. It is a time that rejuvenates and inspires; you ride a wave of hopeful energy as you shift your focus to a direction that boosts your morale. There is an opportunity ahead to learn a new path. You don't need to hesitate, you can take a chance and be bold, as it is a powerful option that eliminates doubt and uncertainty. The crux of this journey lies in your willingness to maintain flexibility and openness to all possibilities. It brings visionary ideas that tempt you towards a diverse route forward. It does bring improvement to your home life; it is a time of reestablishing a base from which to grow your world. Impressive results are possible, events unfold over the coming months that bring harmony into focus. Your willingness to explore possibilities guides your situation forward. It does bring unusual changes in your life that open a variety of paths to explore. As you develop the potential in your world, you discover a way that nourishes your mind and soul. Expanding your horizons brings new people into your life, while others will fall by the wayside. It's all part of growing your situation and learning valuable lessons that bring essential change. An unexpected surprise touches down in your world soon. The hidden information is revealed, it does light up a path of valuable insights. The seeds you plant blossom into a creative enterprise. It does let you maneuver forward and embrace developing your world.

FEBRUARY WEEK TWO

The New Moon this week does wipe the slate clean on many levels. Your life has undergone many changes, this can feel unsettling. There is a strong emphasis on improving your experience. An invitation ahead offers a diversion that draws abundance. There is an opportunity to mingle ahead. There is energy simmering, and that brings a foundation in love. It involves romantic bonding and developing intimacy with someone who captures your heart. Your emotions run high, and there is a strong desire to merge dreams with this person. It does initiate a phase where growth is possible in your personal life. It brings an enjoyable chapter that removes blocks and opens the path ahead. It kicks off a fresh cycle of growth, it does bring new adventures for your social life. Entertaining and engaging times are spent with a crew of kindred spirits. It does give you a much-needed break from your usual routine and shines the light of potential on personal goals. Your willingness to open your life to new options draws an expansive chapter. The goals you set for yourself are given an avenue for expression soon. It takes you towards a time of ever-widening options that draw in new possibilities. It brings a time that is right for progression as you launch towards developing your vision. Advancement is looming, it does bring valuable potential into your world. It is an excellent time for networking and exploring areas of growth. It does draw a sweet chapter filled with lively conversation. It brings a heightened sense of well-being and does see a time of personal growth coming into focus. Under this powerful influence, you can achieve an active phase of advancing your dreams.

Mercury Retrograde ends at weeks end. Complications are set to fade, it brings the sunshine into your life. An opportunity comes knocking that sees your potential blossoming. It does bring a breakthrough that is a turning point for your life. A great deal of activity emerges that helps you capitalize on your talents. It brings a terrific route towards expanding your consciousness. You are propelled forward towards a journey of promise. This is an incredible time for self-discovery and contemplating the spiritual realm. It does bring the empowering chapter that creates fertile ground that lets your creativity expand out in ever-widening circles. A curious area ignites your interest, it does bring a path that captures your attention. Spreading your wings, you soon expand your abilities into new areas. It is is a pivotal time where you can choose a path that brings abundance into your world. It does harness an element of adventure and excitement, a gateway opens, something incredible is ready to emerge. It brings a track that puts you in contact with other individuals who can provide fresh perspectives. It brings a winning chapter that draws blessings into your life. Changes are occurring in your life. It is all part of evolving your life and making the best possible decisions. It does bring a path that opens new options, these opportunities are sent to advance your life. It does see new potential trickling into your world and bringing newfound possibilities to light that inspire your mind. Staying in sync with your vision does bring prominent outlets for creative expression. It speaks about new horizons, something curious is coming provides you with a path you can embrace.

FEBRUARY WEEK FOUR

The Full Moon in Virgo occurs this week, this can create energy peaks that illuminate and draw clarity. It is a time of generating leads and mapping out the finer details for a journey of growth. A collaborative enterprise draws in-depth discussions and does see you considering an innovative approach. Making smart choices brings dividends and leads to a breakthrough. You discover that new people enter your life for a reason. It does highlight a path that draws abundance into your environment. Your willingness to be open to new possibilities brings dividends. There is an influence emerging that let you follow your heart; it captures the essence of your dreams and helps you go after your vision. It does angle you beautifully towards personal growth. It does mark a bold new beginning in your life that sees you following your intuition. You make a swift decision that initiates a wave of transformation. It does bring progress, there are changes made that create the shift needed to bring the abundance you seek. A fork in the road is ahead, you follow a journey that speaks to your heart, and this leaves you feeling optimistic about the potential possible in your world. You have a beautiful ability to nurture an environment that offers room to progress your life. It does open a gateway that provides refreshing potential. You discover a path that tempts you forward, it does bring a fast-moving environment that enables you to adapt and maintain flexibility over the coming chapter. It brings new options; you are ready to raise the bar and pursue your vision.

March 6 - Mercury Greatest Elongation.

The planet Mercury reaches its greatest elongation of 27.3 degrees from the Sun. If you would like to view Mercury, look for Mercury low in the eastern sky just before sunrise.

March 6 – Last Quarter Moon in Sagittarius.

This Moon phase occurs at 01.30 UTC. –

March 11 – Neptune in Conjunction with the Sun.

The planet Neptune in Conjunction with the Sun. This occurs at 00:00 UTC.

March 13 - New Moon in Pisces.

The New Moon creates space for a new chapter. This phase occurs at 10:21 UTC. This is an excellent time to observe galaxies and stars because there is no moonlight to obscure your view of the universe.

March 20 - Vernal Equinox.

The March equinox takes place at 09:37 UTC. There are equal amounts of day and night throughout the world.

March 21 – First Quarter Moon in Gemini.

This Moon phase occurs at 14.40 UTC.

March 26 - Venus Superior Conjunction.

The planet Venus at Superior Conjunction. This occurs at 06:00 UTC.

March 28 - Full Moon in Libra.

This Moon is on the opposite side of the Earth as the Sun and shall be fully illuminated. This phase occurs at 18:48 UTC. This full moon is known as the Full Worm Moon. Powerful energy lights a path forward. You can attract and manifest excellent results during the complete moon phase.

Mercury reaches greatest elongation this week. This can feel destabilizing, but in fact, it creates a useful change, you move away from destructive influences and create lifestyle changes that draw benefits. The information arrives that takes a moment to digest. It does bring an opportunity that supports a stable phase of growth. There is an outpouring of new energy ready to flow into your world. It brings exciting options that leave you feeling optimistic. There is an element of surprise and excitement, this weekend delivers the news that brings you a boost. This information gets you back on track and leaves you feeling inspired. This is a time that lights up pathways of creativity and self-expression. It does bring an exciting adventure that captures the essence of freedom and liberation. You are transitioning towards a glorious new path. You may feel uncertain about shifting your focus, this is natural, your intuition is guiding the road ahead. It does bring a time that gets you back into the groove of things. Be discerning, use your best judgment, to obtain your highest result. This governs a phase of surrender, being flexible is going to get you where you need to be. It's time to release any blocks which have held you back. These changes might not be as difficult as you fear, you are being guided to keep open to new opportunities which will flow into your world soon. Clearing the decks for the unique potential to arrive helps heighten your ability to choose a path that offers you growth and stability. Writing your goals out will help you focus on tackling the most critical projects which demand your attention. You soon awaken a sense of creativity, which inspires change.

MARCH WEEK TWO

Neptune arrives in conjunction with the Sun this week. The Planet Neptune rules dreams and healing, while the Sun places a strong focus on self-development. The influence of the Sun draws an energizing power that bolsters your spirit. It does bring opportunities to spread your wings, and this empowers and enriches your life. You are shaken out of everyday routines. This has you rebuilding your life from the ground up. It brings new options that fuel a surge of optimism. Building stable foundations in getting back to basics do bring balance into your world. It is restorative and helps you find your groove and take advantage of new areas of potential. It does see you moving in alignment with your heart. Your willingness to be open to new environments is instrumental in bringing potential into your life. It does leave you feeling optimistic, and as you nurture this energy, you can pour your energy into achieving the first phase of growth. You enter a new landscape filled with incredible potential, being aware of long-term goals helps you make the most of this time. Serendipity points the way forward. The fantastic potential is set to be revealed. You draw a situation that brings fortune to the forefront of your life. It begins a beautiful phase of developing a position that speaks to your heart. It does bring meaningful conversations that turn over a new leaf, you bright space for the unique potential to arrive. It does bring exciting changes that draw happiness.

Additionally, the New Moon in Pisces this week sees some unusual changes; it does lift the lid on a new chapter. You channel your excess energy into a creative project, which leads to an epic adventure. Intentions are set at this time, go far, and you see a goal reach fruition the next full moon.

Ostara, the Spring Equinox, takes center stage this week. It's all about facing the sun again after the long winter and starting new plans and goals, you can harvest later in the year. You make headway and embrace a refreshing environment. This is an especially important time to release the past and move towards a new area. It does correspond with developing a meaningful situation, it gives you an inspiring path to focus your creative energy into. Sowing seeds and nurturing their growth leads to an active phase of growth. An open conversation occurs soon. It does bring things up, and this lets you know where you are headed. You are strong, resilient, tenacious, and capable. This will hold you well over the coming weeks. Specific goals you put in place do unfold, and this heartens your spirit. It does begin a fascinating chapter that offers unique pathways to growth. Wisdom from the past has a strong influence over you, and rightly so. You have innate abilities to overcome troublesome areas and harness the power within your intellect. It does see things improving, something is circulating nicely in the background of your life, and this will be revealed in due course. It does bring an option that hasn't fully been developed, you soon have the chance to build your abilities further. Information arrives, which has you feeling as though you have landed on cloud nine. It does translate to an extraordinary chapter where things fall into place. If you have found yourself feeling a sense of discord or out of sorts recently, this is going to release the issues and draw a new chapter, complete with exciting new options. You reveal enticing potential, it paves the way for a beautiful breakthrough to occur.

MARCH WEEK FOUR

Venus sashays into your life this week, it is a time that draws fulfillment. An impromptu social event provides you with a remarkable opportunity, it sets the stage for future get-togethers with someone who inspires your mind. It does draw tranquility and leaves you feeling content.

Additionally, the Full Moon in Libra highlights a time of increasing opportunity, a major makeover is coming. It is a time of wiping the slate clean and starting over. It's the only thing that makes sense during this transformational time. It is a line in the sand that reflects a set point, once you cross over this mark, you reach the dawn of a new era. Intentions set at this time unfold over the coming months and are a trigger for different paths and possibilities to emerge in your life. It does bring moments you can treasure. The future is tinged with magic, it does bring sizzling opportunities that increase the pace of your life. It draws a productive and energetic chapter that catalyzes you to create the change you seek in your world. It does bring noteworthy information that paves the way towards achieving a stable phase of growth. It brings a proactive time that influences your life on many levels. A fruitful mission is ahead. The Stars show an expansive time that brings new activities into your life. It does place focus on long-term plans and a useful task crops up that inspires your mind. If things feel overwhelming at this time, you can appreciate the changes ahead. It does bring clues of new opportunities that surface to expand your life towards an original path. It does heighten the potential possible and marks a significant turning point.

APRIL ASTROLOGY

April 4 – Last Quarter Moon in Capricorn.

This Moon phase occurs at 10.02 UTC.

April 12 - New Moon in Aries.

The New Moon phase occurs at 2:31 UTC. This is an excellent time to observe galaxies and stars because there is no moonlight visible.

April 19 – Mercury at Superior Conjunction.

The planet Mercury at Superior Conjunction. This occurs at 02:00 UTC.

April 20 – First Quarter Moon in Leo.

This Moon phase occurs at 06.59 UTC.

April 22, 23 - Lyrids Meteor Shower.

The Lyrids meteor shower runs each year from April 16-25. This meteor shower peaks on the night of the 22nd and the morning of the 23rd. These meteors can produce bright dust trails that last for several seconds.

April 27 - Full Moon in Scorpio, Supermoon.

The Moon is on the opposite side of the Earth as the Sun and will be completely illuminated. Full Pink Moon. It's the first of three supermoons for 2021. This occurs at 03:31 UTC. The Moon will be at its closest approach to the Earth and may look slightly larger and brighter than usual. Powerful energy lights a path forward. You can attract and manifest excellent results during the full moon phase.

April 30 – Uranus in Conjunction with the Sun.

The planet Uranus in Conjunction with the Sun. This occurs at 21:00 UTC.

Revolutionary changes are transitioning you forward. This lets you break free from the past, you light up a new pathway, it revamps your potential. Restoration of spirit motivates you to chase your dreams. You have a resilient and robust sense that overcomes obstacles and can find solutions to just about anything. You are headed towards a culmination of sorts, and this brings remarkable personal growth into your life. Developing your future brings miracles and magic into your life. You channel your energy towards a path that draws inspiration. It has you moving into uncharted territory. You face a critical crossroads and may have a sink or swim feeling. It does bring a time of planning and following through with actions that take your aspirations further. It brings a fruitful phase that let you emotionally process recent events. Shedding outworn skins and the circumstances that drain your energy does bring a huge turning point. You begin to see challenges as steppingstones to skip along towards a brighter future. It shows a time of personal growth, it involves soul-expanding insights and experiences. You discover a breakthrough moment heralds a new chapter. It does see your heart opening, and this brings a willingness to explore diverse pathways. Directing your attention towards an area that inspires and excites your mind does see you crossing the threshold and transitioning forward. You follow a path of serendipity that leads to your destiny. Harnessing the power of flexibility provides you with a gateway towards your goals. Sensitivity and emotional awareness are blending with your intuition to guide this process forward. A milestone is reached, you create a path ahead towards your vision.

APRIL WEEK TWO

The New Moon in Aries packs a nugget of wisdom. It is a time of excitement, inspiration, and creativity, it does have you dreaming big about future goals. Someone is thinking a great deal about reaching out and getting the ball started on talking online with you. They feel that keeping in touch will be a positive move forward that opens the door towards developing a closer bond. It does seem that secret information will be revealed via a message from this person. Getting involved with developing the situation does bring abundance. It draws a soul-stirring chapter that has you moving into new territory. It brings a landscape that is stable, expressive, and meaningful. You scoop a path of good fortune with this sensitive soul, this individual has a tendency to be a free spirit, they feel excited about the potential possible. It brings an active and busy time in your personal life. Being open to change does draw the time of excitement, inspiration, and romance. It has you dreaming big about the future, a journey of discovery lights up a path forward. It sets the stage for fantastic growth to occur in your personal life. You have been going through a transitional time that can bring up a restless vibe. It does have you contemplating new pathways towards growth, and this sets the stage for a dynamic chapter ahead. Reflecting on the changes that surround you, you resolve to improve your circumstances. It does see an increase in luck and good fortune arriving this week.

Mercury at Superior conjunction this week sees you reaching a crossroads, it can be challenging to know the path ahead when you face a dissecting road. You have a resilient spirit and the know-how to navigate around occasional roadblocks that limit your progress. This is a time that requires essential adjustments to your life. It does bring courage out into your world. You can begin to feel a positive change by harnessing an optimistic mindset. It also offers a chance to communicate on a deeper level, some brilliant ideas spark and brainstorming with others can bring meaningful collaborations into your life. It's an exciting time of sharing and mapping out ideas and thoughts. While there have been some twists and turns in your life, you can see the path ahead open with new options. It does bring new potential into your world, implementing creative strategies draws dividends. You may even discover an original way of learning opens that can be considered a sign. Keeping productive brings a burst of fresh energy into your world. It speaks about adventures calling your name. A sense of wanderlust has you wanting to branch out and bring new options into your life. You discover an entirely new way of dealing with issues. It allows you to put stress to bed and embrace developing a path that speaks to your heart. Setting your sights on a distant goal does bring an inspiring new endeavor to light. You have the green light to connect with your inspiration and harness creative solutions. Getting immersed in areas that make you happy brings joy into your world. There is a positive influence arriving that delivers a boost. It does allow your best qualities to shine as you radiate a dynamic vibrancy.

APRIL WEEK FOUR

The Full Moon in Scorpio is a Supermoon that sweeps into your life to draw closure, healing, and this transitions you forward. Some lovely changes are arriving soon. In fact, something inspirational comes, that makes you smile. A lot is going on, stepping out of the ordinary routine does bring new possibilities to light. It lets you dive into a new environment, and this offers room to grow your spirit. The timing is synchronistic, a path is revealed that adds spice and excitement to your life. You have gained the attention of someone from your outer circle. This is someone who now has time to contemplate the situation at length. Overall, the conditions are changing, and there is a desire to expand their life. It is guiding them to get to know you on a better level and deepen the bond. It does touch you down on a chapter that offers to bring changes into your life. More emotional energy is on the way with this person. Information is revealed that uncovers some remarkable chemistry with someone from your neighborhood. This person is nearly ready to take that leap of faith towards sharing their thoughts with you. Life holds a refreshing time when it draws a moment of discovery with this individual. It does see you blazing a trail towards a more social aspect. Being open to new possibilities does spark a situation of interest.

You can embrace your true talents. You lift the lid on a curious option that brings new possibilities into your life. Information is revealed that sparks a path of discovery. You can embrace the quickening of inspiration. It paints a landscape that is social and enables you to bond with someone who cares deeply about you. Being the recipient of this supportive energy does bring beams of joy into your world.

May 3 – Last Quarter Moon in Aquarius.

This Moon phase occurs at 17.50 UTC.

May 6, 7 - Eta Aquarids Meteor Shower.

The Eta Aquarids meteor shower runs annually from April 19 to May 28. It peaks this year on the night of May 6 and the morning of May 7.

May 11 - New Moon in Taurus.

This phase occurs at 19:00 UTC. The new moon phase is a brilliant time to observe galaxies and stars because there is no moonlight visible.

March 17 - Mercury Greatest Eastern Elongation.

The planet Mercury reaches its greatest eastern elongation of 22 degrees from the Sun. If you would like to view Mercury, look for the Mercury low in the sky just after sunset. This planetary phase occurs at 06.00 UTC.

May 19 – First Quarter Moon in Virgo.

This Moon phase occurs at 19.13 UTC.

May 26 - Full Moon in Sagittarius, Supermoon.

This phase occurs at 11:14 UTC. Full Flower Moon. It's the second of three supermoons for 2021. The Moon will be at its closest approach to the Earth and may look slightly larger and brighter than usual. Powerful energy lights a path forward. You can attract and manifest excellent results during the full moon phase.

May 26 – Total Lunar Eclipse in Sagittarius.

A total lunar eclipse occurs when the Moon passes completely through the Earth's dark shadow or umbra. During this type of eclipse, the Moon gradually gets more mysterious and then take on a rusty or blood red color. This eclipse occurs at 11:19 UTC.

May 29 – Mercury Retrograde begins in Gemini.

During a retrograde period, it isn't the right time to move forward in any practical venture. Be prepared for misunderstandings and miscommunications to be prevalent.

Someone from the past reaches out to share the important news with you. It does take you to an exciting phase where you share discussions and ideas with someone who holds meaning to you. The past with this person is a treasure trove of beautiful memories. It has been a time that marked many changes, growth and self-development have been part of a more extensive process that has flowed through your life. The years have seen you evolve and shift towards a more centered, peaceful path. A blast from the past breezes into your life. This charismatic individual has been thinking about touching base with you for a while. Recent events spur them towards taking a chance and bridging the gap. It does see this one is willing to turn over a new leaf and wants to draw you into their circumstances. It sets the scene for a lively and adventurous chapter to follow. It is a time of change; you discover a crossroads that has you thinking about the past, and the intersection ahead brings a turning point. It does mark a time of shifting your focus forward, drawing new options to light that creates space for a bold new beginning. Change is in the wind, transformation projects a new trajectory is possible. It brings creative outlets that are expressive and lively. There is also a greater emphasis on fun and friendship, a chance to mingle draws blessings. A flight of fancy arrives to bring inspiration into your world. You can take a break and do something just for yourself. Working on a passion project underscores a time that draws abundance into your life. It brings healing and evolution and guides you towards taking a step forward toward a new chapter.

MAY WEEK TWO

The Taurus New Moon this week sees you being flexible, tenacious, and resilient. The future offers room to continue to evolve your life, you gain traction on a new area that inspires your heart. It brings a shift forward into your life. There is a scene forward, which is characterized by the relaxed ambiance and natural tranquillity, great success, fulfillment, and abundance are ahead. There are many enticing options to explore; you are headed towards a time that reinvigorates your spirit and nurtures a meaningful bond. This week speaks of unexpected news arriving, this information comes out of the blue, it provides you with an opportunity to grow your situation and achieve an important goal you have had on the back burner for a while now. Being mindful of the complexities which surround your life does let you move forward in a balanced fashion. You can adjust to the changes which swirl around your environment and stay mindful of growing a path that speaks to your heart. It does take you to a time of healing, and evolution occurs, which helps you reach for a higher level of growth. Creating sustainable plans holds you in good stead. Eliminating doubt expands horizons and creates space for new options to stir up creativity. It does seem you are soon involved with a passion project that kicks off plenty of robust opportunities to explore. Getting clear about the path ahead does light the way forward towards achieving more structure and stability in your life. You soon uncover a hidden gem that takes your talents further.

Mercury reaches greatest elongation from the Sun this week. There is a matter that is on your mind and has been troubling your thoughts recently. Some changes are surrounding your life, which can feel disconcerting. You have the strength of mind to rise above these concerns and follow a path that speaks to your soul. It denotes the gaining of wisdom, the learning of a new way, and this brings the abundance into your life. It could actually bring a valuable journey that maps essential changes ahead. It's important to cut ties with areas that drain your energy. It does bring new leads to investigate, getting involved in developing your life does bring a grounding force into your world. You get back to basics and embrace being a domestic goddess on your home turf. It does have you evaluate what and who you really need in your life. It is a time that harnesses focus and drive; this amplifies your energy and brings you the courage to move into uncharted territory with confidence. It does bring lively escapades, as excitement soon fills the void.

New ideas are looming, which help you take the next step forward. It is an excellent time for releasing outworn areas and creating space for fresh adventures to emerge. It reveals an energizing moment arrives that hits a high note in your life. It does bring excitement about a cutting edge initiative that draws new possibilities to light. Expanding your vision offers a rare opportunity to delve into an area that harnesses the power of your creativity. It does connect you with other innovative types, and this brings valuable brainstorming sessions. Something is coming that brings your life a boost. It does soothe your soul as it brings a happy moment.

MAY WEEK FOUR

This week delivers a plethora of cosmic activity. There is a full moon in Sagittarius, which is also a super moon, and on the same night, a total lunar eclipse. This is a triple magnifying event. But be warned, three days later Mercury retrograde begins in Gemini, this is the mule kick that may just knock you sideways if you're not aware, that it is coming. So what does all this mean for your life? The triple combo event on Wednesday brings changes that spark a new path. You should seek new experiences and keep open to learning areas that trigger your intuition.

Furthermore, during a Mercury Retrograde phase, you are best to do your own thing and not be drawn into any drama. You may be feeling sensitive, and this can bring up memories of the past. Treasure the lessons learned, as it has shaped your current emotional awareness and helps you become the energetic person you are today. Adopting a gentle approach does draw benefits. You can nurture your environment and sustain a fluid and balanced path forward. You may find the changes ahead disconcerting, but know, they are necessary. Although you navigate towards an uncertain future, it does inspire growth, and being open and flexible in your outlook will bring positive energy to your door. Your well-equipped to overcome hurdles and reap the rewards ahead. Some essential changes are coming that can feel unsettling. It does create space to plug into your creativity and honor, developing a path that is in alignment with your higher calling. Stabilizing foundations helps you maintain equilibrium during the time ahead. It is a time of transformation that grows and expands your life.

JUNE ASTROLOGY

June 2 – Last Quarter Moon in Pisces.

This Moon phase occurs at 07.24 UTC.

June 10 - New Moon in Gemini.

This moon phase occurs at 10:53 UTC. This is an excellent time to observe galaxies and stars because there is little moonlight to obstruct your view.

June 10 – Annual Solar Eclipse.

An annular solar eclipse occurs when the Moon is too far away from the Earth to completely cover the Sun, it results in a ring of light around the dark Moon. The Sun's corona isn't visible during an annular eclipse. This solar eclipse is visible in eastern Russia, the Arctic Ocean, western Greenland, and Canada. A partial eclipse will be visible in the northeastern United States, Europe, and most of Russia. This eclipse occurs at 10.42 UTC.

June 11 – Mercury at Inferior Conjunction.

The planet Mercury at Inferior Conjunction. This occurs at 01:00 UTC.

June 18 – First Quarter Moon in Libra.

This Moon phase occurs at 03.54 UTC.

June 21 - June Solstice.

The June solstice occurs at 03:32 UTC. The North Pole will be tilted toward the Sun, which, having reached its northernmost position in the sky, will be over the Tropic of Cancer at 23.44 degrees north latitude. This heralds the first day of summer (summer solstice) in the Northern Hemisphere, the summer solstice is considered one of the most important times of the year for many traditional cultures.

June 22 – Mercury Retrograde ends in Gemini.

You can now move forward with any delayed plans that you have been putting off due to the Mercury Retrograde phase. Relationships should soon improve as miscommunications are overcome

June 24 - Full Moon in Capricorn, Supermoon.

The Moons will be completely illuminated. This moon phase occurs at 18:40 UTC. Full Strawberry Moon. This is the last of three supermoons for 2021. The Moon will be at its closest approach to the Earth and may look slightly larger and brighter than usual. Powerful energy lights a path forward. You can attract and manifest excellent results during the full moon phase.

You have the stamina to stay on top of things during this Mercury Retrograde phase. There may be an influence that is holding you back, something is preventing progress, taking a moment to plan your goals and consciously release areas that trigger doubt, does let you take a leap of faith into a new chapter of potential. You are in a time of transformation. It does forge an original path that helps you achieve more excellent stability in your life. There is some soul-searching involved that brings a few epiphanies around areas that spark solutions. Brainstorming with another does ground your energy and anchor you in a productive chapter where you can begin to put your ideas into practice. It sees you shifting into an active mode. La Luna brings swift news into your life when information is revealed that illuminates the way forward. Stability and security are a focal point that drives your situation forward. It is a time that brings a crossroads, decisive action helps you cross over into a more productive chapter. It does trigger a path that brings a new phase. A change of priorities has you thinking about the future in a new light. If you're feeling confused about your life's direction, you soon uncover information that reveals an exciting possibility for your love life. It does bring a compelling option for your personal life that draws harmony and happiness into your environment. It begins a chapter filled with promise, this charismatic person sparks your curiosity and, indeed, they become a big focus for you ahead. A new beginning arrives that brings a breath of fresh air into your environment. It is the shift forward you have been searching for, taking time to allow this path to unfurl gently in your life does bring nourishment for your soul.

JUNE WEEK TWO

The New Moon in Gemini combines with an annular solar eclipse. Focusing your energy on home life does build a stable and secure foundation. You head back to the drawing board and strengthen your closest ties. It is a time of going back to basics and revisiting the past, it has you engaging in activities that have been on the back burner for too long. It does bring a gateway that draws abundance into your home life. Becoming involved in events around your home life brings a goal into focus. Changes arrive that create a growth-orientated phase. The fires of your inspiration open a path towards advancing your circumstances. Your life is moving towards a new assignment. This makes a big difference in your life as it enables you to have more time to focus on your passions. It brings opportunities to improve your situation, and this culminates in a time of expansion.

A sunny aspect arrives in your world. You open an avenue that tempts you towards an expansive horizon. It does help you gain traction on your vision; it sees your efforts to improve your situation, gaining momentum. It brings the highly adaptable energy, and maintaining flexibility does let you channel this energy into a productive phase. Something unique is brewing, and this draws a path of knowledge. It links you up with an area that offers a long-term avenue towards developing a goal you have in mind. This is a chapter that connects you to clarity. It helps you blaze a pioneering trail towards expressing your spirit, and it may well trigger a highly creative phase. There is an opportunity ahead that rejuvenates and brings new horizons into your world.

The June 21st Solstice at weeks end is an ideal time to reflect on your goals. There is a new chapter coming which beckons and calls your name. You enter an energizing phase, which enables you to create essential changes. It shows a vital transition occurs that connects you with an avenue you can explore. It does have you developing a pathway that restores your faith in life. It is a time that nurtures abundance, and this brings communication from far-flung areas that may arrive by surprise. Life becomes an adventure, disruptions no longer hold you back, you take everything in your stride and use your imagination wisely. The landscape ahead broadens, it does bring a new terrain to explore. This activates creativity, your sense of innovation is off the charts. As you power up solutions to any problems that crop up, you forge a compelling path forward. It does revolutionize your life, and it brings an essential journey of self-discovery that empowers your spirit. It is an appropriate time to expand your circle of friends. New options arrive for your life. It does draw an avenue that captivates your attention, it brings ambition and opportunity into focus. Plotting a course diligently and with forethought does align you to a path that aids in the ascent of growth. It is a fortunate time to explore new options. Taking concrete steps to improve the bottom line does bring a successful chapter ahead. There are valuable rewards obtained through your willingness to open a new page. Your accomplishments receive recognition soon. This enables you to capitalize on the potential possible, it takes you to a phase of self-expression and fertility of new ideas.

JUNE WEEK FOUR

Mercury Retrograde ends this week. If you have been feeling disconnected or restless recently, it is a time for restoring balance in your world. News arrives that brings a new adventure to light. It does create space for a memorable, once-in-a-lifetime experience. If you are craving stability, this news offers room to work on your foundations. Time spent on the home front draws abundance and invites joy into your surroundings. You are adept at handling the changes ahead. Using tech to your advantage does create a web of support from people in your life. You can unearth new platforms for exchanging messages, it lets you reveal that things are flexible and fluid. There was always a solution to life's problems. It does bring a more human-centered experience into your world. You may be feeling as though you are on an emotional seesaw. Events conspire to trigger your sensitivities, but you can take heart, as things will even out soon enough. Taking a broader approach draws balance and equilibrium into your surroundings. You may also discover some new interests take shape. Things are shifting forward, it does bring new opportunities to work on your life and develop pathways towards growth. It brings a more expressive note into your life. Your vision of what is possible may be changing, but that brings new possibilities to light that pave the way towards an incredible journey. You are on a mission to make the most of life. It does bring options to improve security, building stables foundations leads to a chapter that is grounded and fulfilling.

July 1 – Last Quarter Moon in Aries.

This Moon phase occurs at 21.11 UTC.

July 4 - Mercury at Greatest Western Elongation.

The planet Mercury reaches greatest western elongation of 20.6 degrees from the Sun. If you would like to view Mercury, look for Mercury low in the eastern sky just before sunrise. This planetary phase occurs at 20.00 UTC.

July 10 - New Moon in Cancer.

The New Moon draws rebirth and new energy. This moon phase occurs at 01:17 UTC. This is an excellent time to observe galaxies and stars because there is no moonlight visible.

July 17 – First Quarter Moon in Libra.

This Moon phase occurs at 10.11 UTC.

July 24 - Full Moon in Aquarius.

The Moon is located on the opposite side of the Earth as the Sun and will be fully illuminated. This phase occurs at 02:37 UTC. This full moon is known as Full Buck Moon. Powerful energy lights a path forward. You can attract and manifest excellent results during the complete moon phase.

July 28, 29 - Delta Aquarids Meteor Shower.

The Delta Aquarids meteor shower peaks on the night of July 28 and the morning of July 29. The first quarter moon may block many of the fainter meteors this year. You should still be able to view some brighter ones. Best views should occur after midnight. Meteors radiate from the constellation Aquarius but may appear anywhere in the sky.

July 31 – Last Quarter Moon in Taurus.

This Moon phase occurs at 13.16 UTC.

Mercury at Greatest elongation this week brings unique vibrations. While this is a time that puts roadblocks in your way, but you can overcome obstacles and refine your outlook. It does bring a chance to create new pathways towards growth. Adopting a broader perspective helps bring your energy to an outlet that inspires you creatively. A process of grace and flexibility bring new possibilities into focus. It brings new demands on your life. And while these responsibilities can feel demanding at times, it brings a chance to grow your skills, and you soon develop a cohesive plan that builds a stable foundation. It shows a strong focus on friends and family. It is a time that sees you pulling together and focusing on achieving the best results. It does bring foundations that help you join forces with others, with everything changing so quickly, thinking about structure and planning for the future is beneficial. Some exciting changes are coming up for you. You get support from a more full circle of friends, this sees stress levels halved, it improves your overall well-being.

Additionally, the next significant aspect is a time which sees you let loose with friends, this is a trailblazing chapter where you can enjoy a lifestyle which offers rejuvenation and happiness. A flow of positive energy soon arrives. This brings the gift of security. It does bring valuable resources that have you exploring new possibilities. You sharpen your mind and get creative with innovative thinking. It does bring essential changes that open a path forward. It does see power and strength arrive to deliver a boost. If you have found your energy flagging recently, this brings inspiration, which leads to a productive environment.

JULY WEEK TWO

The New Moon in Cancer this week signifies a new beginning. News arrives, which initiates a wave of potential flowing into your world. Simplicity, at its essence, is a significant contributor to drawing stabilizing energy during this particular time. It also underscores a willingness to adapt and remain flexible, opening your heart to new pathways does bring creative solutions. You discover enterprising activities that lighten your heart and bless your life with new options. You find out about an area that draws abundance. It is a time of heartfelt connections and lively discussions. Processing recent events do release emotional triggers, communicating with a trustworthy person who offers support. Many signs and serendipity are likely to also arrive over the coming chapter. Something special is brewing in the background of your life. New information is discovered that draws a path of abundance. It does bring developments that sow the seeds for future progress. If you are feeling stuck, you can break the cycle and leap into a new path that offers pearls of wisdom. It is a creatively, potent time that expands the barriers of your life. You stay open to fresh ideas and new possibilities, this shines a light on increasing optimism and joy in your world. You have struggled with specific areas and healing those sensitive aspects of your heart lead you towards finding purpose and potential. Crafting your goals during this time could bring a wave of possibility into your world. You touch your deepest desires, setting in motion a sense of manifestation which works in the background to help bring you the right opportunities to sink your teeth into.

It is an unsettling time where many rapid changes can leave you feeling frazzled. If the stability in your life has suddenly turned to quicksand, it is an opportunity to pull back, restructure, and re-organize your life. Getting back to basics does tone down the stress levels, it brings a path with new options. There is a theme of improving circumstances ahead that allows you to adapt to the changes surrounding your life and make lovely progress. This is a time that creates space to focus on developing areas that bring new possibilities into your life. It denotes a time of learning and growth, it does bring new options for learning into your life. A path ahead set all kinds of potential into motion. It does bring news that lights the way forward with forwarding momentum. Maintaining a flexible approach helps you adjust to essential changes. It is an extraordinary time. Indeed, it shows that life is about to get exciting. There are adventurous changes ahead, it does see you embark on a journey that is fluid and changing. It brings new possibilities to light, it pushes back the barriers of your life. Finding your balance in this ever-changing environment does bring the chance to connect with new pathways towards growth. Circumstances align to provide you with heightened social opportunities. There is a secret being kept that once discovered, lets you know someone on a deeper level. This person tends to be enigmatic, they are mysterious and can distance themselves from real intimacy. This outlier does have hidden thoughts about you. They see you as someone enticing, and you have sparked the curiosity. They tend to keep an eye out for you and are currently looking for an opportunity to bridge the gap and get to know you better.

JULY WEEK FOUR

The magic of the Full Moon arrives to put you in a contemplative mode. Nurturing your environment is essential, you can focus on areas that heal your spirit, a vision of the past may impact you significantly during this time. Information reaches you that let you branch out into an area that's been on the back burner for some time. Information is revealed that helps you remove blocks, it offers a path that highlights growth and stability is possible. You soon awaken to a sense of abundance that gives you the information needed to move forward. It is a time of communication, you begin a dialogue that brings honest and open thoughts. Having this person open the heart and be transparent with you helps the barriers lower, it clears the deck for a new chapter of potential with them. Collaborating with others gives you the green light to unload any troubles. In fact, a great deal of supportive energy is arriving soon. It does hold you in good stead to handle a changing environment. A happy chapter brings new possibilities to light. It brings contact with a valuable mentor, and it gives you space to recalibrate your emotional slate. It is a time of growth and personal initiatives that draw dividends. Information is discovered that sends life into an upswing. It brings an auspicious chapter that enables you to transform your world by removing areas that limit progress. Focusing on a path that offers room to develop your personal vision does bring a vital phase of growth. It sees your motivation rising on the horizon, and it is a uniquely uplifting chapter. You cultivate your creativity and bring new opportunities to light.

AUGUST ASTROLOGY

August 1 – Mercury at Superior Conjunction.

The planet Mercury at Superior Conjunction. This planetary event occurs at 14:00 UTC.

August 2 - Saturn at Opposition.

The beautiful ringed planet Saturn will be at its nearest approach to Earth and will be illuminated by the Sun. This planetary event occurs at 05:00 UTC.

August 8 - New Moon in Leo.

This moon phase occurs at 13:50 UTC. This is an excellent time to observe galaxies and stars because there is no moonlight to obstruct the view. A new chapter awaits an open heart.

August 12, 13 - Perseids Meteor Shower.

The Perseids meteor shower runs each year from July 17 to August 24. It peaks this year on the night of August 12 and the morning of August 13. The Perseids meteor shower is usually excellent viewing as the meteors are so bright and numerous. The moon sets early in the evening, leaving dark skies for what could be a unique show. The best viewing is from after midnight.

August 15 – First Quarter Moon in Scorpio.

This Moon phase occurs at 15.20 UTC.

August 19 - Jupiter at Opposition.

The Giant planet Jupiter will be at its nearest approach to Earth and will be at it's brightest. This planetary event occurs at 23:00 UTC.

August 22 - Full Moon in Aquarius, Blue Moon.

The Full Moon draws clarity and illumination. This phase occurs at 12:02 UTC. Full Sturgeon Moon. This year it is also a blue moon. This event only happens on average once every 2.7 years, giving rise to the term, "once in a blue moon." There are three full moons in each season of the year. But as full moons occur every 29.53 days, occasionally a season contains 4 full moons. The additional full moon of the season is known as a blue moon.

August 30 – Last Quarter Moon in Gemini.

This Moon phase occurs at 07.13 UTC.

Saturn at opposition this week brings the energy that is diligent, persevering, reliable, stable, patient. You see life with a fresh perspective, it does release the anxiety, the passage forward suddenly opens as you set your sights on achieving something spectacular. This speaks of a significant transformation taking place in your life. As you enter your inner sanctum, you touch base with a high level of self-awareness that enables you to see your life from a new perspective. It draws healing and acceptance around areas that may have been buried, and this lifts the burden. Positive influences are coming to your life that illustrates a heightened sense of security in your environment. It shows social ties improving; it brings lively communication. Options are arriving to move social events to a different environment, it does carry activities that help you engage with a broader circle of friends. It's a time of self-expression, creativity, and personal growth. You draw potential into your environment and sweep away areas that are no longer relevant. It has you in touch with a more profound vision. You benefit from events on the horizon. A new page opens in your book of life, it has you initiating a path that inspires your mind. A fresh approach brings a new initiative; it gives you a time of growth. You undertake an essential phase of learning that brings wisdom and experience you can bank for future use. You set yourself free by your willingness to be open to change. Prominent areas of your life are calling, and this brings exciting potential into your social life. Your desire to be flexible and fluid does expand the barriers; it brings nourishing energy into a situation that does offer room to heal the past.

AUGUST WEEK TWO

The New Moon in Leo this week begins a new chapter. News arrives that cracks open a new chapter. You begin to see someone in your social circle in a new light. This person is remarkably supportive and highly valuable in this changing environment. You put their talents to good use and begin to lean on them more often. It does draw lively discussions, and these constructive dialogues bring solutions as well as offer valuable insight into the path ahead. There is someone in your more full social circle that has become focused on you. This person seeks to find the right moment to express their feelings. It never seems quite the right opportunity, and now things have moved up a notch, they are thinking about you often. They send a supportive message. You have attracted the attention of an admirer. It does having this person want to build stable foundations. They are focusing their attention on creating chemistry. They rely on your positive feedback before developing the situation.

Further, they are looking for signs that you are also into them. You set their heart ablaze with inspiration, they are looking for the right time to share their secret attraction with you. Someone is holding a candle for you, and they are hoping to find the right moment to reveal their thoughts to you. This person hails from your more full circle of friends. When you can take advantage of opportunities to socialize, you will discover they move forward and begin sharing thoughts and ideas with you. This person seeks to focus on developing a closer friendship before moving into uncharted waters.

There is a restless vibe that can feel disconcerting, it does bring change. Still, you can adjust to a fast-moving environment with the right mindset. Being flexible opens the floodgates to a flow of grounding energy that restores balance. It is an unsettling time, but you reach a turning point and creates space for releasing all that stands in your way between your perception and a state of happiness. If things feel unsettling, know that you can soon anchor your focus in an ambitious goal. It does ground your energy as you discover the pace and rhythm of your life picks up. A positive transition occurs that is the result of your willingness to open your life to new experiences. It does see you dive into uncharted territory and come out a winner. If things feel sensitive, this is set to ease as your stability increases. It is a time of having to readjust expectations. You must follow your intuition and trust that things will come together when the time is right. There are a lot of benefits to be gained by using this time wisely and creating space to nurture your home environment. It draws stability and security into your life, this grounds your energy and does create a fantastic foundation you can use to restore your spirit. You reveal enchanting information, it does promote an avenue that draws harmony into your life. A secret is shared with you that brings a personal situation into focus. Being open and willing to expand your life brings a new realm of possibilities. It puts you in touch with a liberating sense of freedom; you pass a threshold towards a brighter future. The attention you give to this does provide the opportunity to stabilize the foundations and create a more secure environment. A serendipitous path forward opens and paves the way for a new chapter.

AUGUST WEEK FOUR

The Full Moon in Aquarius at the beginning of this week is also a rare blue moon. There are some lovely changes set to flow into your life. A new understanding enters your world, which is restorative to your energy. Life offers new areas of growth and learning. Now is the perfect time to act and broaden your horizons by exploring possibilities that inspire your mind. Letting your imagination run wild does bring new options, it is a beneficial process that sets the stage for future progress. A great deal is ready to be unveiled, and it may have you diving into an eclectic path. It does bring a sense of a manifestation that lets you draw abundance into your world through a combination of innovation and creativity. It does seem harmony is ready to emerge in your life. It brings new possibilities into your love life like that helps you move forward towards achieving a personal goal. It does show your life is sparked by new potential, it enables a bond to develop and become closer. It speaks of transformation that enriches your love life, it also indicates you should remain committed, focused, and proactive about achieving your vision. Something you hope for does come to pass. It does spark positive change; it rules a path that sweeps abundance into your life. It gives you a chance to follow your passion and obtain a goal that is close to your heart. There may be some essential adjustments involved, but the critical thing to remember is that these changes are necessary for the full potential to be revealed. Stability and security are at the foundation of this vital process.

September 7 - New Moon in Virgo.

The Moon is on the same side of the Earth as the Sun and will not be visible in the night sky. This phase occurs at 00:52 UTC. This is an excellent time to observe galaxies and stars because there is no moonlight visible.

September 13 – First Quarter Moon in Sagittarius.

This Moon phase occurs at 20.39 UTC.

September 14 - Neptune at Opposition.

The giant blue planet will be at its closest approach to Earth, and its face will be illuminated by the Sun. This event occurs at 08:00 UTC.

September 14 - Mercury at Greatest Eastern Elongation.

The planet Mercury reaches greatest eastern elongation of 23.8 degrees from the Sun. This event occurs at 04:00 UTC. This is the best time to view Mercury. Look for the planet low in the western sky just after sunset.

September 20 - Full Moon in Pisces.

The Moon is on the opposite side of the Earth as the Sun, and its face will be fully illuminated. This phase occurs at 23:55 UTC. Full Corn Moon. This moon is also known as the Harvest Moon. The Harvest Moon is the full moon that occurs closest to the September equinox each year.

September 22 - September Equinox.

The 2021 September equinox occurs at 19:21 UTC. The Sun shines directly on the equator, creating equal amounts of day and night throughout the world. This is also autumnal equinox in the northern hemisphere and is considered a significant zodiac event for many traditional cultures.

September 27 – Mercury Retrograde begins in Libra.

During a retrograde period, it isn't the right time to move forward in any practical venture. Be prepared for misunderstandings and miscommunications to be more prevalent.

September 29 – Last Quarter Moon in Cancer.

This Moon phase occurs at 01.57 UTC.

Surprise news leads to an offer that lets you step out of your comfort zone and mobilize your talents in a new direction. It allows you to evolve into a new pathway of growth and learning. Nurturing your inherent gifts enables your fundamental abilities to develop. It brings a journey that is inspiring and trailblazing. It connects you with others who forge a community around a common interest. An opportunity arrives, that allows you to broaden your horizons. It does release restrictions and helps you enter a phase of heightening potential. An opportunity opens that sees you diving into a new role. You can embrace the change ahead as it encourages growth and learning. It's the ticket to an exciting chapter that keeps you feeling active and busy. It brings new people into your life that touches your heart. It seems a business goal comes to life that sparks your interest. It's a time that kicks off a chapter of rejuvenation. It brings opportunities to build your foundations from the ground up, and consequently, this sees you improving your home life. You may discover your creativity goes through the roof; it does bless you with a chance to take your artistic gifts to a new level. In fact, some attractive avenues are arriving soon to keep you busy.

Additionally, there will be a chance to revisit the past and draw healing energy into your surroundings. Life is getting a reboot, you hit your stride in a new chapter of potential. It does bring grounded energy that helps balance and smooth out the issues which have held you back. You're on track to reveal improvement over the coming months.

SEPTEMBER WEEK TWO

Neptune at opposition occurs at the end of this week. Neptune rules your house of dreams and healing. It is a time for reflection, choices are made that get you back on track. It marks a time of significant improvement that brings a shift forward. Flexibility is essential as this assists the navigation required to adapt to the changing environment ahead. The tides are turning, it does bring a positive influence into your world. It speaks of a change that sweeps away negativity, this releases blocks, it points the way forward toward a direction that could come as a surprise at first. You are guided to think outside of your usual thought patterns and look for innovative solutions that encourage growth and self-expression. Your imagination hums with ideas and inspiration, it does symbolize a seed that germinates into a blossoming path of creativity. It does bring an awakening that has you make a breakthrough where you see clearly see why your way is taking you in a new direction. It brings learning and growth that takes you off the beaten track. It does connect you with an expansive world of opportunity. This gently opens the gateway towards a happier environment. There is something in the pipeline, it's likely to have you riveted, it motivates change. It is a lovely time that brings gifts and good fortune. You focus on improving your circumstances, this brings a new project around your home. Life slows down, the pace pulls back, it brings a gentle flow of abundance that settles your emotions and provides you with stable foundations. A new method that is applied draws an advantage, it helps you get the job done, and you soon start thinking about the next area to tackle.

You are given a boost when you notice synchronicity is guiding the path ahead. It creates a shift for your emotions that brings a positive and refreshing essence. This helps you quiet, restless vibrations, you get a greater sense that things are going to work in your favor. More balance and stability emerge, it does create the right environment for life to flow forward. An offer crosses your path that sparks your interest. You hear whispers of a new role and reveal an exciting possibility that makes a dramatic entrance into your life. It guides the path forward and broadens your horizons. It links you with like-minded individuals. Overall, the landscape ahead is expanding, this tempts you to dive into a new area. A random conversation with another sparks this diverging path. It is a time of planning that has you thinking about the future in a new light. You open a new book of chapters as happiness appears radiantly on the horizon. It puts you in contact with those who help improve your life. Advancing a goal that is close to your heart does wonders for your spirit. Digging deeper provides the breakthrough; it sets a pace of growth and self-development. Things are shifting towards change, it is a time that draws refreshing options. It brings an avenue that glitters with potential. Taking down your barriers lets you harness a sense of manifestation. It does bring new territory to dive into. You gravitate towards an area that develops your life. It brings a stimulating and active environment that leaves you feeling enthusiastic about future possibilities. It does allow you to push your boundaries back and enter a game-changing chapter of discovery.

SEPTEMBER WEEK FOUR

The Equinox this week speaks of a golden opportunity arriving to inspire your mind and shift your focus forward. You illuminate fantastic potential, a time of abundance, and magic is looming. It does bring a phase of strong growth, it's a time that is highly expressive and lets you blaze a trail forward towards an adventure that calls your name. It rewards your courage with an unexpected bonus. Information arrives to encourage your continual evolution on this path of growth. You cast your net wide and discover a fascinating passage forward. The timing is superb, and the avenue opens that reveals new options. It does bring a role that elevates your abilities to a higher level. It takes you on a journey that lets you open your life to new experiences. A leap of faith initiates terrific changes. You overcome setbacks and bounces back quickly, keeping your eye on the target does bring a cycle of growth that leads you forward towards making gains. Your situation is currently changing and evolving. It does let you move forward correctly. You soon enter a phase that highlights the achievement of a goal that is close to your heart. You attract the assistance of another who also supports your life. It does bring a happy chapter where you can forge ahead and begin to see progress occurring. It brings a time that is lighter and more buoyant. You are ready to make a move forward. Structuring your goals lets you take in new avenues of growth. It does bring a time where you expand your abilities and grow your talents. You may currently be sorting out precisely which role to take, something new is coming that gives you a snapshot of where your abilities can take you. It is a peak season for creativity and innovation.

October 6 - New Moon in Libra.

The New Moon speaks of something new arriving in your world. This moon phase occurs at 11:05 UTC. This is an excellent time of the month to view galaxies and stars because there is no moonlight visible.

October 7 - Draconids Meteor Shower.

The Draconids meteor shower runs annually from October 6-10 and peaks this year on the night of the 7th.

October 8 – Mars in Conjunction with the Sun.

The planet Mars in Conjunction with the Sun. This occurs at 04:00 UTC.

October 9 – Mercury at Inferior Conjunction.

The planet Mercury at Inferior Conjunction. This planetary event occurs at 16:00 UTC.

October 13 – First Quarter Moon in Capricorn.

This Moon phase occurs at 03.25 UTC.

October 18 – Mercury Retrograde ends in Libra.

You can now move forward with any delayed plans that you have been putting off due to the Mercury Retrograde phase. Relationships should soon improve as miscommunications are overcome

October 20 - Full Moon in Aries.

The October full Moon is on the opposite side of the Earth as the Sun and will be fully illuminated. This phase occurs at 14:57 UTC. This full moon is known as the Hunters Moon. Powerful energy lights a path forward. You can attract and manifest excellent results during the complete moon phase.

October 21, 22 - Orionids Meteor Shower.

The Orionids meteor shower runs yearly from October 2 to November 7. Orionids meteor shower peaks this year on the night of October 21 and the morning of October 22.

October 25 - Mercury at Greatest Western Elongation.

The planet Mercury reaches greatest western elongation of 18.4 degrees from the Sun. Look for Mercury low in the eastern sky just before sunrise. This event occurs at 05:00 UTC.

October 28 – Last Quarter Moon in Leo.

This Moon phase occurs at 20.05 UTC.

October 29 - Venus Greatest Eastern Elongation.

The planet Venus reaches its greatest eastern elongation of 47 degrees from the Sun. This is the best time to view Venus. Look for the bright planet Venus in the western sky after sunset. This planetary phase occurs at 22.00 UTC.

OCTOBER WEEK ONE

Mercury retrograde delivers a message about finding balance within the hurricane. If you feel troubled by uncertainty, know that you will soon see the bigger picture. It does give you space to reflect, and this helps you process any emotions which limit your true potential. Releasing baggage brings healing. It lets you set your future intentions correctly, once you have your goal in mind, there is little to prevent you from achieving a stellar result. This is an especially appropriate time to release the past and move towards joy and abundance into your life. You can sow the seeds and nurture them to develop an inspiring path. Channeling your creative energy into an area that resonates positively in your life will draw stability and happiness. It does let you take hold of an opportunity and amplify the potential possible. You are gifted with a lovely sense of compassion and empathy; you have a splendid ability with animals. You can improve your situation by exploring new areas and embarking on an adventure that inspires your spirit. There is potential coming that is likely to arrive in waves, each option more curious than the previous. It takes you on a path that offers growth, learning, and wisdom. You work hard to create a stable foundation, the efforts you undertake are fundamental in drawing harmony and security into your life. It is part of a more extensive chapter of growth that lets you head towards your vision. It does bring a diverse journey, and it enables you to gain abilities and refine your talents over time. You learn through trial and error how to make the best of whatever environment you land in.

Mars, in conjunction with the Sun this week, lets you pop the cork on the genie's bottle. A decision is required to move forward and reach for the progress you are seeking. Pausing to reflect on the changes which swirl around your life, you can gain a more comprehensive perspective. It does see you need to go beyond your current comfort level and expand your boundaries into new territory. You benefit from the work you do and enter an emotionally rewarding chapter, it takes you to a more abundant landscape. It does bring a personal goal into sharper focus soon. It places a spotlight on a journey that inspires your heart. Circumstances are set to shift, and this creates an environment where you can nurture and develop an alliance. Advancing a personal goal is a top priority, it has you opening a new door and kicking off an exciting chapter. As you gain a better understanding of the path ahead, you move towards a brighter chapter. It places you in the box seat to resonate with the right frequency to take you forward towards a phase that draws abundance into your surroundings. It does see an expansion occurring that guides you towards a journey that glitters with new possibilities. It is a time that energizes your spirit and inspires your heart. You find a proper direction to channel your energy into. This elevates your mood and creates a shift that draws abundance into your world. It is a time of closing the door to painful memories and opening a fresh chapter forward. Firing up your creative energy lets you pinpoint a path that sparkles with inspiration. It brings an essential time of advancing your vision and diving into something worth your time.

OCTOBER WEEK THREE

This is a time that grows your world. Constraints are lifted when Mercury Retrograde ends this week; your situation expands outwardly. An avenue opens that brings a necessary change; it has you thinking about the possibilities. It dramatically shifts your focus towards an area that holds promise. It is a time that brims with potential, you scope out a path that offers you room to you use your abilities to stunning effect. You tap into a journey that inspires your mind, and it has you feeling focused and busy as you begin to structure your goals forward. There happy moments that arrive to balance and bless your life. It does bring more stability into your world, and there are some lovely surprises ahead that bring a boost to your life soon.

This Full Moon in Aries brings emotional awareness. The past is a time of many treasured memories that tug on your consciousness to cause you to reflect. This helps integrate current changes, and it draws balance and stability into your world. In fact, something is coming that gives you an excellent sign that you are on the right path to developing your life. Surprising news lights up areas of inspiration and creativity. It brings a boost to your life. It is a time where the opportunity comes knocking. There are rewards on offer if you broaden your perception and stay clued up to signs that tempt you forward. It does have you knowing precisely when to take the reins of an enterprising chapter. If you have found the energy recently was feeling disruptive, this is set to smooth out. It is a time that sees you working smarter and conserving your emotional reserves.

You find opportunities to join forces with others who support your journey forward. It gives you a leg up on creating an environment that brings stability into focus. You can broaden the scope of your imagination and harness creativity to stunning effect. Growth and learning are highlighted as a valuable accessory during this time. This is someone you share common ground with. There is a spark that could certainly ignite chemistry if given a chance. Fanning the flames of desire does see a closer bond emerging with this person. It's all about reconnecting with him and getting the opportunity to engage in a more intimate conversation. Setting positive intentions is a powerful way to begin a process of manifestation. You stay true to your spirit with this person, it does have you digging deeper. Sometimes the path isn't as clear-cut as you would like it to be, yearning for companionship invites this person into your life. It does bring quite a shift of potential, focusing on developing a new chapter with this person gives you a fantastic direction to channel your energy into. It does lead to inspiring conversations and a meaningful moment. It does seem an exciting possibility leaves you feeling enthusiastic. It speaks of a refreshing change coming; it does bring a stable and calming influence into your life. It releases the uncertainty and doubt that has felt disquieting recently. It brings a path that guides you forward by allowing you to trust in the process and let go of fixed expectations. It broadens your perception of what is possible, and it brings a lofty vision into focus.

NOVEMBER ASTROLOGY

November 4 - New Moon in Scorpio.

The New Moon brings a clean chapter of potential. This phase occurs at 21:15 UTC. This is an excellent time to view the stars because there is no moonlight visible.

November 5 - Uranus at Opposition.

The blue-green planet will be at its closest approach to Earth, and its face will be fully illuminated by the Sun. This event occurs at 00:00 UTC.

November 11 – First Quarter Moon in Aquarius.

This Moon phase occurs at 12.46 UTC.

November 12 - Taurids Meteor Shower.

The Taurids meteor shower runs yearly from September 7 to December 10. It peaks on the night of November 12.

November 17 - Partial Lunar Eclipse

A partial lunar eclipse occurs when the Moon passes through the Earth's partial shadow or penumbra, only a portion of it passes through the umbra. During this eclipse, part of the Moon darkens as it moves through the Earth's shadow. This partial lunar eclipse will be visible throughout most of eastern Russia, Japan, the Pacific Ocean, North America, Mexico, Central America, and parts of western South America.

November 17, 18 - Leonids Meteor Shower.

The Leonids meteor shower runs yearly from November 6-30. The Leonids meteor shower peaks this year on the night of the 17th and morning of the 18th.

November 19 - Full Moon in Taurus.

The Full Moon is on the opposite side of the Earth as the Sun and will appear fully illuminated. This phase occurs at 08:58 UTC. This full moon is known as Full Beaver Moon. Powerful energy lights a path forward. You can attract and manifest excellent results during the complete moon phase.

November 27 – Last Quarter Moon in Virgo.

This Moon phase occurs at 12.28 UTC.

November 29 – Mercury at Superior Conjunction.

The planet Mercury at Superior Conjunction. This planetary event occurs at 05:00 UTC.

NOVEMBER WEEK ONE

The New Moon in Scorpio this week brings insight, clarity, and awareness. Healing is fundamental to making progress. If you find yourself feeling sensitive or emotional, prepare to enter the current path of abundance. Give yourself the space necessary to adjust and maintain a flexible trajectory. It is a changing environment that lights up new pathways towards growth. Focusing on areas that inspire your mind helps to smooth over any rough edges during this time of transition. This reboots and restarts your environment on many levels. It does see creativity burning brightly in the background of your life. You can harness the power of this energy to develop pathways that head towards growth. A vision is arriving, and this brings a path that glitters with golden opportunities. It does bring awareness that you are shifting to a new and unfamiliar environment. Immersing yourself in areas that bring you joy does enable you to ground and center your energy. There is an emphasis on everyday practical matters, deal with the situations which currently surround your home life. Slowing down may be of help; it draws balance and let you plot a course towards a grounded chapter. You receive new information soon that brings good news. While it does drive essential changes, it enables you to navigate the path ahead and delivers a more stable environment. It does see you making headway on a goal that is dear to your heart. Life has put the brakes on, but you can create space for a fresh chapter to emerge. Initiating new projects sets plans into motion that unfold into a path that inspires and delights. You can manifest your own happiness and progress in your abilities.

The Taurids meteor shower, which peaks on November 12th this year, see your potential shine brightly. Your star is rising; it's an exceptional time to plot a course towards a lofty endeavor. A new doorway appears and tempts you forward. It does bring a valuable turning point you can embrace. You can take matters into your own hands, don't wait for fortune to come knocking, as you can create your own magic. It does bring a favorable time where you can upgrade your vision and go after a truly spectacular goal. It does let you shine in a creative area; you can embrace developing your talents and dive into an assignment that inspires your mind. You can reach for more as it is a time that opens your life to a new flavor. A variety of pathways tempts you towards new activities that connect you with diverse characters. You discover fantastic options that draw improvement into your surroundings. It does bridge the gap between your dreams and tangible outcomes. You soon make your mark on a vision that holds promise. A path of adventure that transitions you forward towards a journey of great hope. It does direct your abilities towards a remarkable opportunity. As you launch forward, you release limitations that hold or block your progress. It does enable you to strengthen your life and improve your circumstances. You can release outworn areas and clear the decks for new possibilities to arrive. A message arrives that inspires your heart. It does see significant changes coming that help you build a stable foundation with another. Deepening a bond does begin the process of opening your life to another. A new chapter is coming to set your heart ablaze with inspiration. There is movement ahead for your personal life.

NOVEMBER WEEK THREE

A Partial Lunar Eclipse on the 17th brings a landmark moment, it is a gateway toward a brighter future. This Lunar Eclipse speaks about a second chance. You may notice recurring themes in your life that hark back to an earlier time. It is all part of a more full resonance of energy that lets you deal with what is currently happening by utilizing the wisdom of the past. Unexpected change brings an opportunity that enables you to break free of the current restrictions. Something curious is unfolding in the background of your life, you are well-advised to adopt a wait-and-see approach, so things are revealed in due course. Riding a wave of hopeful energy, you shift direction and follow a path that lets you negotiate unseen waters, it brings a time that rejuvenates and inspires. A valuable resource opens that enables you to see the road ahead clearly. It involves a discussion with a person of interest and may have you entering a new venture. It brings an essential time of following your intuition and exploring pursuits that raise the bar higher and deliver impressive results into your world. It does release the pressure as you achieve an excellent outcome. News arrives out of the blue that opens a new path. It suddenly clears the way forward and brings a new option that offers exceptional results. It does see you contemplating exciting possibilities and exploring a new role. It can add concrete stability and security to your life. It brings a lift up for your career path and does carry a boost you can appreciate. The energy you resonate with is so very grounded and stable, and this sees improvement arriving on the home front. It illustrates how you can create your own magic.

Reflection and contemplation of valuable tools that help clear sensitive feelings. It is a favorable time to release blocks and focus on building grounded and stable energy on the home front. In a timely coincidence, you received news of an area that sparks with potential. It is a journey that illuminates a path forward, and you can embrace developing your vision in this direction. You can resolve areas that hold you back as changing your mindset flings open the door to abundance. It does get things flowing forward. Motivation and inspiration blend to make a potent brew of potential. It lights a compelling way where you can dive in and embrace making the most of the situation at hand. You are entering a changing cycle that can feel jarring, keep working through your emotions to reach the other side. Hidden information shall be revealed. It gives insight into areas that are best released. It does release blocks and resolves outworn regions that hold your real potential back. It enables your vision to expand, it brings new energy and opens a box of magic. The seeds you plant blossom into a productive cycle that launches your abilities toward a higher realm of possibilities. This is an ideal time to prove your worth and show everyone how you can achieve great things, even when under pressure. You rise to the occasion and utilize the talents of resourcefulness, creativity, and innovation to achieve your highest result. It does reward you with tangible results, it brings stability into focus and let you make a snap decision that is on the ball. Things are set to improve. You have specific skills and expertise to share with a broader audience, and this bestows your life with a sense of abundance. Your wisdom is beneficial to another.

DECEMBER ASTROLOGY

December 4 - New Moon in Sagittarius.

The New Moon brings a clean slate of potential. This moon phase occurs at 07:43 UTC. This is an excellent time to view galaxies and stars because there is no moonlight visible.

December 4 – Total Solar Eclipse.

A total solar eclipse occurs when the moon completely blocks the Sun, revealing the Sun's outer atmosphere, which is called the corona. The path of totality will, for this eclipse, be limited to Antarctica and the southern Atlantic Ocean. A partial eclipse will bee visible throughout much of South Africa.

December 11 – First Quarter Moon in Pisces.

This Moon phase occurs at 01.36 UTC.

December 13, 14,15 - Geminids Meteor Shower.

The Geminids meteor shower runs each year from December 7-17. The Geminids meteor showers peaks this year on the night of the 13th, 14th, and 15th. The nearly new moon this year will provide dark skies for an excellent show. Best viewing will be from a dim vista after midnight. Meteors will radiate from the constellation Gemini but can appear anywhere in the sky.

December 19 - Full Moon in Gemini.

The Full Moon illuminates and draws clarity. This moon phase occurs at 04:36 UTC. This full moon is known as the Cold Moon and the Moon Before Yule. Powerful energy lights a path forward. You can attract and manifest excellent results during the full moon phase.

December 21 - December Solstice.

The 2021 December solstice occurs at 15:59 UTC. The South Pole of the earth tilts toward the Sun, which, having reached its most southern place in the sky, is directly over the Tropic of Capricorn at 23.44 degrees south latitude. This December solstice also marks the first day of winter in the Northern Hemisphere.

December 21, 22 - Ursids Meteor Shower.

The Ursids meteor shower occurs each year from December 17 - 25. This meteor event peaks this year on the night of the 21st and morning of the 22nd.

December 27 – Last Quarter Moon in Libra.

This Moon phase occurs at 02.24 UTC.

DECEMBER WEEK ONE

December hits the right kind of positive note that you need in your life. It is a favorable time to upgrade your dreams and chase your vision. Kindred spirits figure strongly into the weeks ahead. It does see you unwinding with your social circle, a celebration or significant social moment arrives to rejuvenate your life. It brings a valuable sense of belonging, security, and stability. It does bring foundations that involve bonding and the merging of dreams. As you engage with new options in your social life, you enter an exciting time where you connect with another who energizes and enlivens your world. It does bring shifting priorities, change arrives that guides your progress forward. As you evolve and grow your vision. There is a strong sense of renewal and rejuvenation taking place. This is a time that is a catalyst for change; summoning your faith, you can embrace a chapter of excitement and adventure. It does bring new pathways towards growth, it lets you harness your sense of adaptability and flexibility. It connects you with areas that offer you new skills and abilities. It does see you sharing experiences with someone who brings you joy. This is a time that governs increasing stability on the home front. It does rule getting back to basics and overcoming obstacles with a shift of perception. This takes you towards a path that has you making your own opportunities from the ground up. Your imagination and creative thinking are rising to meet the challenges you face. You put your unique stamp on the world. Your innate curiosity continues to seek expansion. You strike the right balance between progress and tradition this month.

A time of rejuvenation is coming that revitalizes your spirit and gives you a glimpse of future possibilities. It does strengthen and deepen your reserves. Taking time to appreciate the level of growth you are going through does ground you in an environment that is ripe with blessings. It is a time that offers pearls of wisdom; the work you undertake creates a shift that brings a myriad of opportunities into your world. This is a time where you can do your very best work. It's a highly innovative and adaptable phase that lets you flex your muscles of creativity to stunning effect. Your imagination is humming along with incredible ideas that stoke the artistic fires that burn within your soul. There is an incredible underlying energy that seeks an avenue of expression. Any sacrifices you make during this unsettling time are going to hold you in good stead. It does elevate your life and brings growth and wisdom to the forefront of your life. It ultimately leads to more responsibility on your shoulders, you undergo a test of strength, knowledge, and determination, and rise to meet the challenges head-on. There is good news arriving on your doorstep soon. Watch out for news that comes to bring a boost to your life. It does have you contemplating this information through a new lens of perception. It sees a development occurring that draws stability on the home front. It is a significant focus of that delivers such good news and a path forward. It is a necessary time that lets you shift your focus towards new goals. Getting involved with your wider community does bring the most exceptional personal growth. It does bring a shift forward that transitions you toward a chapter that offers room to grow your life.

DECEMBER WEEK THREE

Some personal goals are coming to fruition soon. It does have you seriously contemplating the path ahead and taking time to focus your energy on developing a situation that leaves you feeling enthusiastic about the prospects possible. It connects you with a broader world of opportunity, this places you in the box seat to expand your life and deepen the ties which bind. An influx of social engagements arrives to support a broader phase of personal growth. It is a time that brings peace and joy, it also offers exciting news which shows up in a flurry, creating quite a stir. It is an exciting time for singles to explore new options in your love life. The forecast is enticing, a social aspect provides you with an unusually vibrant phase which offers you room to mingle with like-minded individuals. This takes you to an active chapter with an abundance of opportunities. Casting your net wide will see you enter an expansive phase, you indeed can stoke your ideas and put plans into action. This is a substantial time for you to take decisive action towards obtaining a goal. It may be the initial steps towards working towards the achievement of something extraordinary or taking action to reach for your dreams. It does bring a lighter chapter; this allows you to expand your horizons and double your creativity. It is a time that favors you beautifully. It showers gifts and luck and has you developing your goals. This gives you a fabulous start, which genuinely does boost your options this week. As you explore, new possibilities open to tempt you forward. This chapter reflects the sunshine which seeks to come into your world. You enjoy an excess of social invitations which enable you to spend time with refreshing characters.

You are set to enter an optimistic chapter, it offers you options to circulate, this social growth does inspire a light-hearted environment. It has you spending time with friends and family. It stirs terrific conversations with others, it draws blessings and abundance into your life. It gives you plenty to ponder and contemplate as you consider enticing options. It is best to stay objective, look at the broader picture, and discuss your options. You benefit from taking a flexible approach, there are many new options ready to emerge, your life is changing, and this draws plenty of opportunities into your world. You discover a magical aspect ahead, which makes you happy, that is a lovely area to focus on. You to joyously reconnect with an old group of friends, this draws abundance into your world and begins a reflective cycle, as you explore treasured memories of the past with them. Don't be surprised if a photo album is brought out in this quick process. Your spirit is guiding you to broaden your horizons. A spontaneous adventure brings you in contact with like-minded individuals. Overall, the landscape ahead is inspiring; it takes you towards releasing emotional baggage and unleashes you in a vista which tempts you to explore new experiences. You entered a time of focusing on yourself and exploring new beginnings. Projects which hold passion take center stage, and you find the clarity and motivation to develop your life. Tapping into your creativity releases anxiety and negativity. This is a crucial process that allows loose ends to dissolve and enables you to look forward to some beautiful moments which seek to arrive in your world this week.

Dear Stargazer,

I hope you have enjoyed planning your year with the stars utilizing Astrology and Zodiac influences. My zodiac star sign books are released each year, which detail a monthly list of astrological events, and a unique weekly (four weeks to a month) horoscope. You can find me on my Facebook page where you can get personal astrology or intuitive readings.

https://www.facebook.com/SiaSands

Instagram: SiaSands

See my full list of books here:

https://www.SiaSands.com

Leaving a review is welcomed and appreciated.

Many Blessings,

Sia Sands